Mary Ann's Best of Helpful Needlecraft Hints

edited by

Susan D. Cole

illustrations by

Gerri Sorkin

Published by
Craftways Publications

A division of
Craftways Corporation
Berkeley, CA 94710-1374

This book is dedicated to needlecrafters of all ages, around the world, -- whose works have brightened so many lives.

Copyright ©1981
Craftways Corporation
1465 Fourth St.
Berkeley, CA 94710-1374

ISBN 0-9607224-0-8

Library of Congress 81-68620

First printing November, 1981

Second printing January, 1982

The Best of Hints for:

Introduction

Whether you're a beginner or an experienced needlecrafter, this book was designed for you. It's chock full of hints, facts, and creative ideas that will make your needleworking hours easier, faster, more pleasant and rewarding. We've sifted through thousands of needlecraft ideas to select what we feel will be most useful to you. We've arranged them by craft for quick reference.

Most of our hints use materials found in a needlecrafter's home. Our other hints use items readily available from your local craft, drug, or hardware store. We hope you will find this book to be of great value and will refer to it often.

The hints and general information contained in this book are tested suggestions only. The editor and publisher can not guarantee results. We recommend care, patience, and pretesting whenever possible.

The Best of Hints for
KNITTING &
CROCHET

Don't let your problems get the "worsted" of you!

Yarn selection -- wool or synthetic?
* Wool is warm even when wet. Generally it is available in a wide range of muted colors. It may require special care in cleaning. It blocks to fit. Some people may experience skin irritation and other allergic reactions.
* Synthetics (acyrlics, nylon, etc.) are usually machine washable. They are generally non-allergenic and are available in a wide range of colors, especially the brights. They may stretch and grow.

Is it wool or synthetic?
* If you have leftover yarn and wish to know its content, try the flame test. Cut a short piece of yarn, put it in an ashtray, set it on fire. Wool will burn to an ash, synthetics will leave a hard residue.

What's a "ply"?
* Ply refers to the number of strands of yarn twisted together to make the yarn. Individual strands are twisted together to strengthen the resulting yarn. Ply has nothing to do with the weight of the yarn -- there are lightweight 4-ply yarns, and heavyweight 3-ply yarns. Knitted worsted is a 4-ply yarn.

Match your dye lots
* Buy all yarn for your project at the same time -- checking the "dye lot." Yarn is dyed in batches. Non-matching lots may be different shades. Save your original yarn labels in case you must order more.
* If you run short of yarn for your project, and can't get more in the same dye lot, add a stripe of a contrasting color. This will look much better than if you try to finish your project with a yarn that doesn't quite match.

Preparing the yarn

* Yarn purchased by the hank needs to be formed into a ball. You can have someone hold the hank on outstretched hands while you wind the ball.
* Or, slip the hank over the back of a chair.
* Remember to loosely wind the ball so that the yarn will not lose its elasticity.

Winding yarn into pullout balls

* Wind hanks of yarn evenly around a flattened cardboard core of a toilet tissue or paper towel roll. Leave tube in place until you're ready to work. Pull tube out, locate inside end of yarn, pull, and start work.

Don't get unraveled

* You can prevent the ends of metallic yarns from unraveling as you work if you first dip them in clear fingernail polish.

Cleanliness

* Plastic bread wrappers or produce bags are excellent for keeping yarn clean as you work. Slip the skein into the wrapper. Cut a small hole in the bottom of the bag, feed yarn through. Seal open end of bag with rubber band.

Gauge

* Did you know your gauge can vary day to day depending on your mood? Tense, your stitches may be too tight. Relaxed, stitches may be too loose. Check your gauge occasionally to be sure it remains consistent throughout.
* Always make a 4" sample swatch using the needles, pattern, and yarn you will use for your finished project. Carefully measure the swatch before beginning your project and make adjustments.
* If your knitting is tighter than the instructions call for, try knitting with a size or two larger needle.
* If your knitting is too loose, try a needle a size or two smaller.

Tired hands?

* If your hands feel tense, sprinkle talcum powder on your fingers -- the yarn will slip over your fingers more smoothly.

Tangle-free yarn carrier

* Cut off the top of a plastic milk bottle or bleach bottle (thoroughly rinsed). Place ball of yarn in the bottle, run yarn through the handle, pull yarn to use.

8

Rescued yarn
* Use a cake rack for drying unraveled yarn from sweaters, etc. Wrap the yarn loosely around the rack, dip into water, hang to dry. You will have kink-free, tangle-free yarn to rewind.

Easy to follow directions
* Before you start your project, draw a circle around each number throughout your directions which applies to the size you are going to make. If you reuse the directions at a later date in a different size, circle the appropriate numbers with a different color.

Knots
* Always try to join two lengths of yarn at the edge of the garment (rather than in the middle of your work) -- here they can be hidden by a seam or edging.
* Spliced ends look better than knotted ends. Try this -- unravel 1" of each yarn end, interlock strands, twist splice to match the twist of the yarn and work as usual.
* Tie yarn ends with a square knot leaving ends at least 2" long. When your work is completed, work the cut ends into your garment.

Shoulder straps
* When knitting or crocheting the strap for a shoulder bag, make two pieces and join them with fusible web -- this prevents curling and stretching.

9

End washing woes

* Tie a short piece of yarn into the inside neckline or waistline of hand-made garments. Red means no machine washing, green means go!

Boy or girl?

* When making an expected baby's sweater, make buttonholes on both sides of the sweater front. When the baby is born, you or the mother can sew the buttons over the correct side for either boy or girl.

Sewing seams

* Split yarn (use separated ply) whenever possible to make seams flat and dainty.
* Keep the yarn no longer than 18" so it will not become weakened.
* Pin seams using the plastic pins used in brush hair curlers. They work better than straight pins because they won't slip out of place, are rustproof, don't snag, and are longer!

Threading ribbon

* You will find it easier to insert ribbon into your knitted or crocheted garment if you first wrap a piece of tape around the end of the ribbon.

Blocking tips

* Always use rustproof pins when blocking.
* Use cold water to wash, never oversoap, rinse thoroughly several times.
* If you leave the pieces very wet it will be easier to make them conform to the measurements.
* Always support the garment when lifting it from the water, so it won't stretch.
* Since acrylic yarns may stretch permanently when steam blocked, proceed carefully. Pin the garment according to the measurements required. Steam, cover with a damp cloth, and allow to dry.

Drying knitted garments

* Lay your knitted garment on heavy absorbent towels to dry in an area where there is good ventilation. Change the towel under the pieces twice a day.
* Never place knitted garments in the sun to dry -- they will fade.

No more itch

* Wool garments will be less itchy, and softer, if rinsed in cool water with a few drops of glycerine added.
* The sleeves of a sweater can be lined with the legs of an old pair of pantyhose and you'll have no more itch. Just cut a section of hose to fit and baste into place.

Handy yarn storage

* Use a wine rack for holding skeins of yarn.
* Or, cardboard boxes for qt. beverage bottles (from the supermarket). You can paint to match a room's decor.

Handy needle storage

* Crochet hooks and short knitting needles can be stored in an empty fireplace matchbox. They come in a wonderful selection of designs and colors.
* Or, in an empty potato chip can.
* A piece of plastic webbing (like you use for outdoor furniture), can be folded in half horizontally with 4" extra on one end, stitched or stapled together along the vertical edge, and thereby made into a sturdy case.

Don't rely on memory

* Save a 4" knitted or crocheted sample swatch of every garment you make in a binder or index file. Add comments about the finished garment. Later projects will benefit from your good recordkeeping.

Gift wrapping

* When giving a crocheted or knitted gift to a friend, include a bit of leftover yarn for mending, and the yarn label with its washing instructions.
* Or, wrap the package with some of the leftover yarn and your lucky recepient will have a bit of yarn for future repairs.

Proper packing or storage of garments

* Lay a skirt out flat, place tissue paper on top, fold twice -- horizontally.
* Lay a dress out flat, place tissue paper on top. Lay the sleeves over the top of the dress. Fold dress horizontally, dividing into thirds.
* Fold a coat in the same manner, except make only one fold.
* Lay a sweater out flat, place the tissue paper. Fold sleeves over the front, make one fold bringing the bottom up to the top.

It's best to be sitting while knitting!

Choosing the stitch pattern
* The garter stitch (knitting every row) stretches equally vertically and horizontally.
* The stockinette stitch (knit one row, purl the next) stretches more crosswise than lengthwise.
* The seed stitch (knit one stitch, purl one stitch; the next row: purl one, knit one) stretches like the garter, but is firmer.
* The ribbing stitch (knit one, purl one) is very elastic in the crosswise direction and is therefore used where you want an edge to stretch to fit.

Casting on
* A general rule for casting on is 1" of yarn for every stitch.
* Cut the short end of yarn to 5" so it won't get in your way.
* Or, leave it on and use it for sewing the garment together.

Ridges
* Don't leave knitted projects on the needle in one place too long -- a permanent ridge may form. Either work at least one row a day, or when you next take up the work, rip out the row you had on the needle, tie on a new piece of yarn and begin anew.

All about markers
* Plastic price labels from bread wrappers can be used as markers for your knitting.
* Or, tie a short piece of yarn (of a contrasting color) into a circle and use it as a marker. This is especially good when knitting with fine yarns where a rigid marker would cause a distorted line.

Neat trim edges
* When knitting following the stockinette pattern, slip the first stitch onto the right hand needle without working it. Work the remaining stitches as usual. Next row, and all to follow, repeat this process. Your edges will be neater.

Sleeves
* If your sleeves are to be identical, you can put them on the needle and knit them at the same time; this will insure that they will be the same length.

No more stretched out cuffs
* Weave some elastic thread through your knitted cuffs and other ribbed edges to keep them in shape.
* Use needles I or 2 sizes smaller than used for the body of your garment.
* Knit sewing silk of the same color as your yarn into the first few rows.
* Never steam-iron over ribbing, you'll flatten it, causing it to lose its elasticity.

Easy knitting
* Try holding your working needle under your arm, pressed against your body. This allows more freedom of movement with your working hand.

Keeping track of decreases
* A snap fastener can be "snapped" into place to mark increase and decrease rows.
* Or, tally as you go using a child's magic slate. Your knitting needle can do the marking.

Built in ruler
* With a waterproof marker, or fingernail polish, mark your knitting needle every inch from the tip -- a handy ruler.

Yarn holders

* Use a tapestry needle to run a contrasting thread through stitches you want held. Bring the ends together and tie. Make sure the loop is large enough to allow the stitches to lie flat.
* If you use a safety pin as a stitch holder, slip a small button on first -- this will keep the stitches from catching on the spring.

Bobbins

* Form the yarn into a figure eight around your thumb and forefinger. Slip off and secure with a bobby pin.

New life for broken knitting needles

* Sharpen the broken end in a pencil sharpener, smooth with sandpaper. You now have a new double-pointed needle.
* A broken knitting needle may be just what you need for staking up a limp houseplant.

Binding off

* Use the next largest knitting needle in your right hand to prevent the bound off row from being too tight.

Sleeves too short?

* You can lengthen the sleeves or body of a knitted garment quite easily. Remove the cuff, pick up the stitches using a small needle. If the pattern is stockinette, you can work in the opposite direction -- without it showing. If the pattern is something other than stockinette, work in ribbing to the desired length, and then bind off.

It's easy to get hooked!

Smooth work
* Rub paraffin into your hook occasionally to keep it working smoothly. Wash it in soapy water.

Garment edging
* Edging cloth with crochet? First stitch around the item with an unthreaded sewing machine. The large holes will make it much easier for a small crochet hook to slip through.

Crocheted rugs slipping?
* Attach rubber jar rings to the bottom of the rug.
* Or, buy a piece of 1/4" foam rubber (available at the five and dime) the size of the rug and slip it underneath.

Crochet hook storage
* Store crochet hooks in a plastic toothbrush holder -- especially nice when traveling.

The Best of Hints for
CREWEL

It's a "crewel, crewel" world!

The meaning of the word
* 'Cleow" (of Anglo Saxon origin), became "Clew", which became "Crewel" -- meaning "ball of thread."

No more tangles
* Wind the yarn around your fingers. Slip the yarn into a plastic price tag from a bread wrapper. Mark the color number on the tag with a waterproof felt tip pen.
* Use strips of upholstery tape (which is two narrow strips of tape with spaced snaps) to hold your colored-sorted yarns.

Only draw the graph once
* To enlarge patterns draw squares on lightweight cardboard; tape waxed paper on top. Draw the design with a felt tip pen. Remove the waxed paper and use for your pattern. The original squares are unmarked and can be used again.

Using a hoop
* It's almost always better to use an embroidery hoop or frame. A taut fabric will make work easier, make stitches neater, and prevent fabric from being pulled unevenly by the embroidery.
* If your background fabric is too small for your hoop, baste strips of torn sheeting to the edges -- this will extend the edges of the fabric.
* Remove your embroidery hoop after your day's work because dirt will collect around it -- leaving a ring.

A free-standing hoop
* Work goes more quickly and easily on a free-standing hoop because you learn to work by "stabbing" the needle in. One hand always stays on top, the other underneath.

Stretcher bars

* Use stretcher bars when working on a loosely woven fabric -
  - a hoop may distort or stretch the fabric.

Applying design for crewel

* Break a needle in half, put the blunt end into the eraser of an
  ordinary pencil. Place a piece of dressmaker's carbon on the
  fabric; position your design, pin in place. Use the broken
  needle to prick the outlines of the pattern. (An added advantage is that the pattern may be reused).
* A variation of the pricking method for applying a pattern is to
  use the sharp needle to outline the design, then rub "ponce"
  (a fine powder) over the holes. Remove the pattern, blow
  away the excess powder, connect the dots with a dressmaker's
  pencil, or a fine paintbrush.

On sweaters

* Loose weave fabrics require another method for applying
  designs. Trace design onto tissue. Baste in position on right
  side of garment. Embroider through paper and fabric, when
  done, remove paper.
* Or, trace design onto a transparent material (such as chiffon).
  Pin the material to wrong side of garment. Baste outline of
  design using contrasting thread. Embroider on right side of garment over stitches. Clip away any excess chiffon.

Protect fragile fabrics

* When embroidering on velvet and other fragile fabrics,
  protect the fabric. Place a piece of tissue paper over the
  design, put the whole works on a hoop, tear away the excess
  paper, and begin your work.
* Tissue paper also keeps stitches that lie under the hoop from
  being flattened.

Which needle to use

* Use crewel needles (sizes 1-10) for most embroidery. They
  are sharp-pointed, short, and especially good for "stabbing" up
  and down.
* Use chenilles (sizes 13-26) for embroidery worked with
  heavier yarns. They are sharp, and are thicker and longer than
  crewels.
* Tapestry needles (sizes 13-26) are blunt. They do not split
  threads and are useful for weaving (traveling) on the surface.
* To weave a few stitches with a sharp needle, push your needle
  eye first through the fabric.

Using crewel yarn

* Crewel embroidery yarns can be stored and used in the plastic cans 35mm film comes in. Punch a hole in the top of the can, roll the yarn into a ball and feed it through the hole.

Consider the use

* The type of use, and the amount of use, that an item will receive is an important consideration when selecting yarns, fabrics, and stitches for a project. For example, a chair in the dining room will receive more wear than a pillow in the guest room.
* A tightly twisted hard yarn will wear better than a loosely twisted soft yarn.
* Stitches on chairs and other upholstered furniture should be kept short -- long stitches can catch. However, long stitches can be anchored.

Washing crewel

* Often your crewel will become soiled from handling. If it is washable, wash it with a mild soap in a basin of cool water. Never rub. Rinse thoroughly. Place in a towel and blot excess water.

Pressing

* If piece is to be pressed, lay it face down on two layers of towels. Cover with a dry press cloth. Press the embroidered area gently never setting iron down on section -- just touching press cloth. Press the surrounding fabric as usual.
* If the fabric is dry at the time of pressing, use a damp press cloth.
* If a fabric is not washable, spot clean (first testing on a hidden edge), or send to a dry cleaner.

Blocking

* If your crewel has become misshapen, it will need to be blocked.
* A small piece of crewel can be blocked in a hoop; sprinkle with water, leave in place to dry.
* A large piece of crewel can be blocked using stretcher bars.

Preparing a blocking board

* Select a piece of pine or pressed wood somewhat larger than the finished piece of crewel. Cover the board with muslin -- wrapping fabric to back and stapling or tacking in place. Mark muslin into 1" squares (a grid) using a waterproof pen. Place embroidery face up or down according to the texture of the stitches. Tack corners in place. Tack sides each inch to measurements. Let dry completely.

Protect Stitcheries

* Spray stitcheries with a fabric guard to prevent them collecting dust and grease.

The Best of Hints for
CROSS STITCH
&
EMBROIDERY

Keep yourself in stitches!

Handling embroidery thread
* To insure better coverage separate all strands of embroidery floss before using. Then put back together the number required.
* Separate embroidery strands easily. Cut a length of embroidery floss. Pull it across a dampened sponge. Moistened, the strands will easily separate, then dry in seconds.

How many strands?
* How many strands you use is determined by how large the "X" you are going to cover.
* Use one less strand for your backstitch than you use for your cross stitch.
* Cut strands to 18" lengths so they won't wear thin from being pulled through the fabric.

A "knotty" problem
* Don't knot ends (unless it's on a garment that will often be washed). Leave 3" of yarn on back and cover with later work.
* Or, run the thread under 4 or more stitches on back of work.
* Don't carry dark threads under unworked areas of a light fabric. The threads will show through the completed project.

Don't get caught up in your work!
* Wind embroidery thread onto knitting bobbins (available in your art needlework department) and you will have no more messy tangles.
* Keep threads untwisted so they'll lay flat and not fray. Occasionally stop your work long enough to drop your needle and thread so they can unwind.
* To keep threads from catching, keep hoop adjustment screw in 10:00 position (1:00 if left handed).

Metallic threads
* Dip ends of metallic embroidery thread in clear fingernail polish to prevent unraveling.
* When embroidering with metallic threads, use a needle larger than usual so the hole it makes will allow the thread to pass easily, without fraying.

Working cross stitch
* Find center of fabric by folding it in half horizontally and vertically. Mark spot with straight pin. Each square of design equals one stitch. Start work at center point. Work all cross stitch first, then do outline and other finishing stitches.

Lemons to lemonade
* Spot on your favorite blouse, hole in your best blanket? Embroider a flower around the hole. The hole becomes the center, the embroidery shapes the petals.

Choosing a fabric
* Select a fabric with a linen-type weave -- such as wool, cotton, burlap, or linen.

Needles and yarns
* Choose a needle small enough to slip through the fabric without distorting the weave, large enough to hold the yarn and not squeeze it.
* The yarn and needle should "fit" the fabric, too large a needle or too thick a yarn and the fabric's weave will be distorted. Too small a yarn will appear out of scale on the fabric's surface.
* Store your cross stitch needles in the plastic cans that 35mm film comes in.

Caution!
* Use dressmakers' carbon and pencil where the design will cover them -- sometimes they don't wash out!

The Best of Hints for
NEEDLEPOINT

There's a "point" to these hints!

Choosing a canvas
* Judge the quality of the canvas by the evenness of the mesh and the regularity of the threads.
* Needlepoint canvas is selected by mesh size. #18 has 18 threads to the inch, #12 has 12, etc.

Quickpoint, gros point?
* 20 mesh to the inch or more is considered petit point, 14-18 is called needlepoint, 8-12 is called gros point, and 5-7 is quickpoint.

Mono, penelope?
* There are three major groups of needlepoint canvas -- mono, leno, and penelope.

Mono
* Mono canvas is a single threaded canvas with all meshes uniform in size. It has no up or down; the meshes are evenly spaced. It is easy on your eyes.

Leno
* Leno looks like mono, but actually it has two threads running parallel to the selvage edge that are twisted to hold one thread running perpendicularly.

Penelope
* Penelope is an interwoven canvas with double horizontal threads intersecting double vertical threads. It has selvages and a "right" way to be worked.
* Penelope is versatile -- you can work petit point and gros point on the same canvas because you can separate the threads. It is a good choice where the design has many curving lines.
* Good penelope canvas has a distinct up and down ripple. Cheap canvas looks flattened -- and the threads are much more likely to break during blocking.

Plastic canvas
* If you are making an item that should remain rigid -- a tote bag, a Christmas ornament, a door stop, you should consider using plastic canvas.
* Plastic canvas is very good for children to practice with.

Work in a frame
* With inexpensive canvas, you will lessen the need for blocking if you use a frame.

Which direction is up?
* Always place your needlepoint design so that the canvas selvages are at the sides, not top and bottom. The needlepoint is stronger that way.
* You can tell which way is up by examining the weave. The pairs of threads across the canvas are slightly more separated than those running up and down.
* Bind the edges of your canvas with masking tape to prevent fraying and to prevent the yarn catching on rough edges.
* Tape the top of the needlepoint with a colored tape, the other sides with plain masking tape, and you will know when picking it up which side is the top.
* Or, write "top" at the top.

A tea party?
* White cotton or linen canvas can be dyed with a solution of ordinary hot tea. The stronger the concentration, the deeper the color. Steep I-3 teabags in a cup of hot water, brush on canvas. Block, and dry canvas.

Designing on canvas

* When marking needlepoint canvas with a pencil, pull the pencil rather than push -- you'll find it much easier to stay on the line.
* If you are not certain the paints you have used on the canvas are waterproof, spray the painted canvas with an acrylic spray before you begin work.

Setting down the canvas

* Always roll, rather than fold, the canvas when you put it down -- this will prevent weakening the canvas.

Estimating the yarn requirements

* Select a yarn suited to your canvas. Work a 1"square in the stitch you will use. Note the amount of thread used. Count the number of square inches you will cover with each color. Multiply the square inches by the yardage to the yarn.
* As a general rule, the diagonal or continental stitch will need 38 square inches per ounce of Persian yarn to cover. With crewel yarn, about 45 square inches per ounce.

Selecting the yarn

* Select a yarn and strands that will cover the canvas well, but not distort the mesh.
* A thread is the full yarn from the skein, a strand is the separated ply.
* Persian is a long-wearing 3-ply yarn, with strands easily separated. It is available in more than 400 colors in lengths varying from single threads 33" long to 8 ounce skeins.
* Tapestry yarns are 4-ply; the strands can be separated but not as easily as Persian's. Generally sold in 40 yard skeins. Tapestry yarns are more widely available than Persian, but in fewer colors.

Worsted's the worst

* Worsteds and other knitting yarns should not be used for needlepoint because their soft, short fibers fluff up and break easily.

"Tweeding"

* If the wool in a kit seems like it may run short, try this. Separate your yarn strands and substitute one strand of a closely color matched yarn for your original. This "tweeding" will extend your yarn inconspicuously.

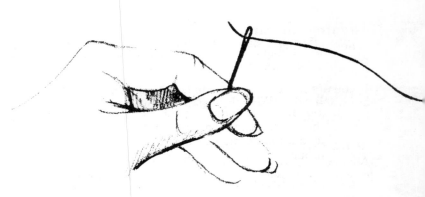

The stitches

* There are dozens of needlepoint stitches but the most commonly used are the "tent" stitches -- diagonal stitches over one canvas mesh. Tent stitches include the Half-cross stitch, the Continental, and the Diagonal (also known as Basketweave).

The Half-cross

* Half-cross stitch works quickly and saves yarn, because there is little yarn on the back. It is useful for pictures and other items receiving little wear.
* When working half-cross stitch work one row, when you come to the end turn the canvas 180° and continue. The canvas will become distorted but can be blocked.
* The Half-cross stitch should be worked on Penelope canvas because it is less stable, may shift and not cover on single-threaded canvases.

The Continental

* The Continental stitch uses more yarn because it covers the back of the canvas. Its added durability makes it suitable for upholstery, pillows, etc.
* The Continental also should be turned 180° at the end of each row.

The Diagonal

* The Diagonal stitch takes the same amount of yarn as the Continental, covers and reinforces the back of the canvas. It is therefore the best choice for chair seats and other items that will receive lots of wear.
* The Diagonal will not require turning at the end of the rows.

Bargello

* Bargello is a general name applied to needlepoint design worked in a straight stitch. It is usually done over 2-6 horizontal canvas threads. It is fast.

Choosing the needle

* When you are selecting a needle, keep in mind that the needle should be large enough to hold the yarn without squeezing, but not so large as to distort the canvas mesh when pulled through.

Check for colorfastness

* Check your yarns, especially imports, for colorfastness. Dampen a small length of your brightest colors and rub them on a white fabric. If they bleed, you know that you should not get your needlework wet.

Which direction to go?

* Work half-cross stitch starting at the upper left hand corner unless directions specify otherwise.
* Work Bargello from the center of the design and work to sides. Then work the background canvas from side to side.
* Work a painted pictorial in this order -- light colors, dark colors, outlines, fine detail, and finally, the background.

A sticky problem

* When moving from a dark color area to a light, or vice-versa, stray fibers may get caught. To avoid this, put a small piece of masking tape on the edge of the completed portion.

How to begin and finish threads

* Avoid knots because they may cause a lump in the completed work.
* Start a yarn by holding an inch or so under the work so the first few stitches will anchor it.
* Or, make a knot, start work from the top side a few inches away. When the work is completed, clip all knots, pull ends to the wrong side of the work, and run under a few stitches.
* To end threads, run the ends under a few nearby stitches.
* Never run dark threads under light because the color may show through.

A last step

* Hold your finished needlepoint up to a strong light and examine for, and fill in, any missing stitches.

Oops!

* You've cut a hole in the canvas. All is not lost. Work needlepoint around the hole to within l/2"all the way around the hole. Push the broken canvas threads to the back. Weave broken ends as best you can, tucking ends into the needlepoint on the opposite side. Unravel a couple of long threads from the border of the canvas. Use them for mending the canvas, keeping to the pattern of the canvas. When the work is done, no one will ever know.
* You can sew sections of needlepoint together using dental floss.
* Or, carpet thread.

Thinking ahead

* Weave a few threads of each color into the back of your work and they will go through the washing and cleaning with the rest of the piece. Then if you ever need to make a repair (for a cigarette burn, etc.), the spare threads will be handy and match the originals.

Personalize your needlework

* Initial and date your project either by working the letters into your original design, or by embroidering over your finished project.

Blocking procedures

* Block needlepoint on stretcher bars. Assemble the bars. Attach your work starting with the mid-points. Prevent distortions by alternating sides as you place your tacks; don't tack one side and then the next. Place staples 1/2"all around. Place the stretched needlepoint under the shower, spray with cool water, and let dry.
* Or, you can use a plant mister to apply the water.

Not colorfast?

* If you are blocking a yarn that is not colorfast, sprinkle the needlepoint generously with salt. Wet thoroughly with cold water. Let dry.
* Or, mix 2 tablespoons of white vinegar in a cup of cold water. Thoroughly dampen, but not saturate, both sides of the needlepoint. This will also prevent the inks in your original design from "bleeding."

The Best of Hints for
PUNCH
EMBROIDERY

Put a little "punch" in your life!

The Origin
* Although punch embroidery has become popular in the United States in only the last few years, largely because of improvements in the punch tool, it has a long history. Crude tools have been found in countries around the world -- including Japan, China, Switzerland, Germany, Iran, The Philippines, and Russia. It was brought to the United States by the "Old Believers" -- a sect that fled Russia to escape religious persecution. This community, which still practices many of the old ways, has a large settlement in Oregon.

What is punch embroidery?
* A raised loop embroidery used to decorate clothing, pillows, linens, wall hanging, jewelry and so forth.

What is the technique?
* After the needle of the punch tool is threaded with an appropriate thread, the needle is "punched" into the fabric. The needles are designed to push the thread between the weave of the fabric. As the needle is withdrawn, the fabric closes around the thread and holds the loop in place. There is no need for knots, simply clip any loose ends flush to the surface of the fabric.
* Normal punch needle technique is to work from the backside of the fabric. This puts the loops on the front side.

Reverse punching
* Reverse punching is used when you want a flat texture or non-fuzzy look -- for stems, strings, or as a fill-in. It is worked from the front of the fabric and the loops form on the backside.

For clarification
* The punch embroidery we describe is not to be confused with Japanese punch embroidery. Japanese punch embroidery uses special rayon stretch threads. Regular punch embroidery generally uses ordinary cotton floss or embroidery yarns.

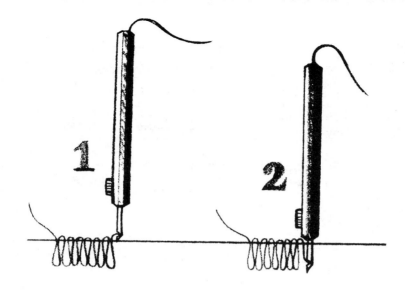

* Punch embroidery uses the same punching technique as rug punches but its smaller needle and tool produce a much finer textured embroidery.
* The most versatile punch needle tools are those that have turn-screw depth adjustment. With an adjustable needle you can produce a wide assortment of textures -- flat, velvet, fuzzy, sculpted, and looped.

Fabric selection
* You can use tightly woven cottons, cotton blends, wools, silks with the small #1 needle. Denim, canvas, and wool flannel can be worked with the medium #3 needle.
* Knits can be punch embroidered if the back is first reinforced with iron-on interfacing.
* However, you may find it easier to punch the design on a woven fabric, then apply the punch work to the knit fabric with a washable fabric glue.
* Needlepoint canvas can be worked with the yarn-size needle.

Fabric problems?
* You should not use worn out fabric for punch embroidery because the fabric will be too weak to properly "hold onto" the embroidery.
* Sometimes the sizing in new fabrics makes punch embroidery difficult. If you encounter this problem, wash the fabric.

Threads

* With a small needle (#1), you can use embroidery floss (1 strand), sewing thread, silk thread, and machine embroidery thread.
* With a medium needle (#3), you can use embroidery floss (2-3 strands), buttonhole twist, #8 pearl cotton, tatting thread, metallic thread.
* With the yarn-size needle you can use embroidery thread (6 strands), #5 pearl cotton, light weight yarns, tapestry yarns, crochet cotton, and some Japanese stretch threads.
* Use a strand, or strands, of thread approximately 36" long.

Hoops

* Metal hoops and poorly made wooden hoops do not hold fabrics tight enough for easy punching. It is best to use a hoop with a screw adjustment.
* Sometimes you can "save" a hoop (make it snug), by wrapping the inner ring with yarn.
* Always stretch your fabric drum-head tight.
* To hold your fabric taut, you should use the smallest hoop possible for your design.
* For larger punch projects (like pillows), it is best to staple your fabric to a wooden stretcher bar frame.
* Or, use an oversize wooden hoop.

How to get good contrast

* Use high contrast colors.
* Outline with short loops (8 mm deep) before you start to fill in a color area (this will also give a neater appearance).
* Or, leave a space between color areas to emphasize the separation.
* Use reverse punching (working from the right side of the fabric). The flat texture will contrast with the looped sections.
* Use both sculpted and non-sculpted areas. Sculpted areas will look about 2 shades darker when cut.

Design

* Study ideas for minatures, jewelry, and clothing in craft magazines, coloring books, greeting cards, and books. Check your local library.
* Look at iron-on embroidery transfers. Many are suitable for punch needle. Follow transfer directions and be sure to apply the transfer to the backside of your fabric.

Creative punching

* Combine threads of different colors in the needle to produce a tweed look.
* Combine traditional embroidery with the punch embroidery. If your design is on the backside of the fabric and you need some lines on the finished side, hold the fabric to a window and trace the lines with a pencil.

Sculpting

* If you want to· add dimension to your punch embroidery, you'll enjoy learning to sculpt. It is frequently used on flowers and flower centers and to simulate animal fur.
* For a smooth sculpted finish, it is imperative that you use small sharp scissors; large scissors tear at the loops.
* Generally the medium sized needle is used, with embroidery floss or #8 pearl cotton.
* Sculpting will be easier if you remove your work from the hoop.
* When working sculpted areas close together, it is better to punch and sculpt one area before going on to the next.
* Remember that sculpting will make the thread appear to be about 2 shades darker, imparting the richness of velvet.

Clipping

* This technique is done on long loops. A couple of rows are punched, the fabric turned over, and with sharp scissors each loop is cut. This is particularly useful for working flowers. For animal whiskers, only one or two punches are required.

What is Hi-Lo?

* Hi-Lo is another technique that looks beautiful on flowers. The center is punched at a low depth, or perhaps sculpted, then each surrounding ring is punched at a higher depth than the one preceding.

Angled shearing

* Is a technique that is particularly useful when you want to create clumps, whether they be grass or thistle puffs. It is a combination of shearing, clipping, and sculpting. Clip open the upper layer of loops. Now lay scissors on top of loops and cut them at an angle, taking off small amounts at a time. This angled cutting will produce gradual layers.

Fringing

* Fringing is especially nice on miniature rugs.
* Fringing is easily done with the medium needle set to its maximum depth. After you have completed your rug design, punch 1 or 2 rows around the edge using #8 pearl cotton or 3 strands of embroidery floss.

T-shirt wearers

* You can use punch embroidery on t-shirts and other stretchy fabrics. Cut a piece of iron-on interfacing slightly larger than the design you are using. Bond the interfacing to the wrong side of the t-shirt. Transfer the pattern to the interfacing, and punch design.

How to personalize clothing

* Use punch embroidery for applying youngster's names on their gymclothes and jackets and you'll lose fewer clothes.

Apply appliques

* Use punch embroidery for making appliques. Transfer the design to your fabric and punch in the normal way. Coat the back of the punched work with fabric glue extending 1/4" beyond the edges of the design. Let dry. Trim away excess fabric. Use a permanent felt-tip marker to disquise the edge of the patch. Glue or sew the applique in place.

Worn cuffs?

* When you apply punch embroidery to the cuffs of work shirts and other clothes that receive hard wear, apply a coat of washable fabric glue to the backside of the embroidery.

It's so quick and easy...

* That you can use punch embroidery as a fast fill in on other types of needlework.

Projects

* Greeting cards are easily made with punch embroidery. Choose a linen or similar weight fabric. Work your design as usual. With your sewing machine, stitch closely (20 stitches to the inch) 5/8" from the fabric edges. Pull threads to form fringe. Using fabric glue, attach fabric to folded card stock.
* The card can later be framed for display.
* A punch embroidery kit, designed to be made into a picture, can also be used in other ways -- fitted around the top of a small box for example.
* Or, with a suitable backing and trim, as a small pillow.
* Or, as a pincushion.
* Flat sections of punch embroidery can be appliqued onto shaped items -- eyeglass cases, toaster covers, checkbook covers, handbags.

Those finishing touches

* Use a dry terry towel to brush away thread clippings from trimmed areas.
* If you apply punch embroidery to needlepoint canvas, be sure to back the finished canvas with fabric glue.
* Washing is good for punch embroidery. The fabric shrinks gripping the stitches tighter.
* Fluff up the sculpted areas of your punch embroidery by washing and machine drying.

The Best of Hints for
MACRAME

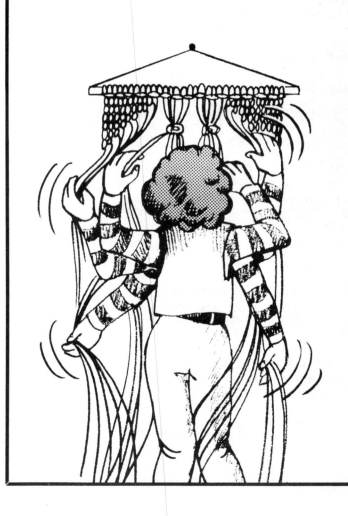

For those "knotty" problems

Slippery problem?
* Nylon and rayon cords will not slip as you knot if you combine them with a fine second cord -- such as wool, cotton, or linen.

The origin
* "Macrame" is from the Arabic migramah -- meaning towel or shawl or the fringe on either.

Mounting surfaces
* Cut styrofoam to the desired size and cover with 1" checked gingham for a handy measuring guide as well as a straight edge.
* Ask at your yardage store for the cardboard from inside bolts of fabric.
* An unused ceiling tile will be handy for working on small projects.
* Fiberboard -- which can be covered with felt if desired.

To get a good grip on the subject
* Use a clipboard.

Adjust your work
* An ironing board's adjustable height can be an advantage.

Press your chairs into service
* Ladderback chairs are helpful with medium length cords. The mounting cord is tied between the knobs on the back of the chair.

From the attic
* A dressform can be used for projects that will be shaped.
* A wig stand is helpful for making hats and necklaces.

Hang it?

* If you use a wire coat hanger to mount your work, you can hang it out of the way in the closet between work sessions.
* Also, you can hang the coat hanger from a cabinet door knob while working.
* If you tie a short cord through the handles of a handbag project, you can hang the whole works from a doorknob while you work.
* You can use an old embroidery hoop as part of a plant hanging project.

Frayed around the edges?

* Dip the ends of macrame cords into clear fingernail polish and beading will be easy.
* Hold a lighted match under nylon cord ends briefly -- they will melt and fuse and you will have no unraveling.
* Wrap the cord ends with masking tape.
* Or, dip cotton cords into melted candlewax.

Lengthy lengths?

* The traditional way to keep cords from tangling, and to keep them short enough to work with, has been to wind each cord around your finger to form a figure eight, and secure the end with a small rubber band.
* You can also hold the lengths with paper clamps.
* Or, twist ties
* Or, paper clips.

As a general rule

* Cords should be cut 8 times what the finished length will be.
* Cords made of a firm fiber can be lengthened by splicing. Cut both cord ends at an angle. Dip both ends into glue. Hold together until glue is set.
* Or, sew the cord ends together, using a matching colored thread.
* Cords of a loose fiber can be spliced by unraveling each end to be joined an inch or so. Overlap the unraveled ends, twist together. Check strength by giving a gentle tug.

Finished?

* When you stain a dowel for a hanging project, use a sponge for applying a smooth coat of stain.

The Best of Hints for
CHILDREN

Kids do the "darndest" things!

Clothes for dolls in dollhouses
* Unless the doll will receive hard use, clothes need not be removable. It is much easier to sew clothes directly onto dolls than to make removable clothing.

Doll clothes
* Using a paper punch, cut disks out of a plastic dishwashing soap container. Use a hot needle to "drill" the buttonholes. Sew wherever you want decorative buttons.
* You can make "ribbon" for doll clothes from any flat woven fabric. Cut a thin strip of fabric, coat the edges with clear nail polish, dry, and apply.

Why add a casing when you don't need to?
* When you need to add elastic gathering to a doll clothes, sew elastic thread through the line you need gathered.

Doll quilts
* Save the foam softener strips you use in your dryer. They make soft batting for dollhouse quilts.
* The foam strips are also useful for padding doll house furniture.
* Old hankerchiefs take on new life in daughter's dollhouse. Those with laced edges or flowered prints are wonderful for bedspreads, curtains, and tablecloths.

Washable toys
* When making children's toys or other items that call for cardboard stiffeners, substitute plastic cut from a dishwashing soap container. Then, if you stuff the toy with foam it will be completely washable.
* When making stuffed animals for children, embroider the eyes, mouth, nose instead of using buttons or beads. Embroidery is safer, longer-lasting, and more colorful.
* Or, use sculpted punch embroidery for eyes, paws, etc.

A quilt for baby

* Select a pillowcase. Cut a piece of batting to fit inside the case. Tuft all layers together. Close the case with a decorative edging or crochet.

* Or, give an old quilt new life. Find a section that is undamaged, cut it down to fit a baby's crib. Bind the edges. Personalize by embroidering family names on the back.

They grow like weeds

* When making pajamas for children, make them a size larger than they need. Put elastic at the wrist and ankle. When they grow, remove the elastic.

* You can lengthen the life of a child's jacket by lengthening the sleeves with knitted cuffs (available from the notions department).

For the child who likes to color

* You can help a child make a colorful poster by pressing transfer patterns onto white paper.

* Or, take several pages, staple them together and make a coloring book.

* Good transfers can be reused up to 5 times in this manner.

Children's embroidery

* Children can embroider pegboard using cotton rug yarn.
* Several children can work on a large piece of pegboard if it is supported on sawhorses or boxes.

How to make a "working frame"

* Children will find their needlework projects much easier to work on if they use a "working frame." Select two pieces of heavy cardboard. Cut the outside edges to size. Cut a "window" large enough to show the child's needlework. Allow at least 1" margin for the frame. Sandwich the fabric between the two pieces of cardboard. Staple every 1/2" all the way around. When the project is completed, the frame can be decorated -- by covering it with adhesive paper or with the child's drawings.

Children's needlepoint

* Children will find plastic canvas very easy to handle.
* Youngsters can learn to needlepoint using a rectangle of metal "hardware" cloth from the lumberyard. Tape the edges with masking tape for safety.

Help children thread needles

* You can make a safe needle for a child to use. Take cotton yarn, spread white glue on about 1-1/2" of one end. Twist to a point. Let dry 15 minutes on waxed paper.
* Or, you can make a needle substitute by wrapping cellophane or masking tape around the yarn.

Threading with soap

* Help children to thread a crewel yarn by using soap. Take two small pieces of soap (or cut a larger bar in two) and set them on the worktable. Have the child put the end of the yarn to be threaded in his mouth to moisten. Put the damp yarn between the pieces of soap (like filling in a sandwich). Press down on soap. Draw the yarn out. The coated yarn should now be stiff enough to thread.

Lock yarn in place

* End the frustration of the yarn slipping out of the needle by locking it in place. Thread the needle as usual. Leave a tail about 5" long. Insert the tip of the needle into the yarn halfway from the end, splitting the yarn exactly in half. Push the needle through -- holding onto the tail so it doesn't also go through. Proceed with your work.

Stitchery

* Limp stitchery is just awful to work on. Prevent burlap and other fabrics from becoming limp by applying spray starch to the back of the fabric, then ironing.

Children and cross stitch

* Have them use a "disappearing ink" pen -- one that washes out of cotton with a water bath (available at craft stores) for drawing the design on the fabric. Following the chart, mark one color of the design at a time. Stitch. Mark next color, work. Repeat process until design is finished.
* If possible, they should work the outline first, then go back and fill in the enclosed area -- that way they won't have to count or look at the graph constantly.
* Have them check off each square on the graph as they go so they can easily keep their place.
* Suggest they work from top to bottom -- the results will be neater.

No frayed edges

* Use pinking shears to trim the edges of work before starting the project.
* Or, tape with masking tape.

Generally speaking

* The smaller the child, the larger the embroidery hoop!

Create sewing cards

* Punch holes in styrofoam meat trays and use for stitchery.

The Best of Hints for
QUILTING, PATCHWORK & APPLIQUE

Fingers are built to quilt!

Cutting shapes
* To keep their shape, any geometric shapes you cut should have at least one side cut on the grain.
* To make lightweight applique pieces lie flat and hold their shape, iron fusible bonding on the back.
* Or, spray them with starch and iron.

Templates
* When cutting small fabric pieces, use an iron-on patch for the pattern. Its coating will keep it from slipping, prevent its fraying, and keep it stiff through repeated uses.
* If you use cardboard templates, put tape on the edges so they won't become worn with use (wear could also change their size).
* Use sandpaper -- which won't slide around as cardboard will.

Chalk talk
* The pattern of a quilt can be marked with chalk.
* Or, with the thin edge of a piece of soap -- which will wash out.

A guide to straight edges
* If you use strips of masking tape to mark the straight lines on the quilt face, you will have no pencil lines to worry about.

Trim selvages from fabrics
* Selvages tend to shrink more than the rest of your fabric and that may cause puckering after the first wash.

Fabric selection
* Use only new fabrics for quilting. Worn scraps will wear out too fast.
* Always choose compatable materials when quilting -- similar in weight and texture. Synthetics tend not to change, natural fabrics tend to stretch or shrink.

Check fabrics for wrinkle resistance

* Crunch a section in your hand -- hold for a few seconds. Release. Does it show wrinkles, or is it smooth -- as you'd like it to look on your bed?

For the faded look

* If you want a faded look to your quilt, wash the quilt fabric with hot water and a little chlorine bleach.
* If you don't want a faded look, test for fading. Cut a swatch of fabric, cover half with a heavy object, and set the fabric in the sun for a week. At the end of the test period, compare the covered with the uncovered section.
* Reds, blues, and purples -- as well as imported cottons, tend to fade fastest and most.

An unusual supply house

* Try your wallpaper store for discontinued wallpaper books that contain fabric swatches.

Fabric storage

* Store your cut squares (pieces) in empty 2 or 3 pound coffee cans. You can keep track of the number of squares by marking on the top of each lid.
* Patchwork pieces can be kept organized! Sort pieces by color and shape. Stack each set of pieces. Run a double strand of sewing thread through a stack, leaving the knotted end at the bottom. Leave the top unknotted. You will be able to pull off the top square as needed. Repeat with each stack.

Notions

* Buy preshrunk yarns, threads, and fabrics whenever possible.
* Or, preshrink items that will later be washed.
* Or, dryclean or steam shrink items that will later be drycleaned.

Cotton batting

* Use cotton batts when you want a flat, smooth quilt. It is easy to sew and handle. Use it for antique, old quilts.
* Because cotton batting shifts, make the rows of stitching no more than 1-1/2" apart, and 9 stitches or more to the inch.

Polyester batting

* Use polyester batts when you want a fluffier, loftier quilt. Use it for modern quilts with polycotton fabrics.

* Because polyester batting shifts less than cotton, the rows of stitching can be up to 4" apart, and 9 stitches to the inch.

When quilting

* Sew with separate up and down motions, or one or two stitches at most -- then pull the thread through. Pulling many stitches through may be faster, but it weakens the thread.

Machine applique

* To make perfect machine applique, sew once around with the machine set for a slightly narrower width than your finished width will be. Then set the stitch width to the final width, and restitch.
* To avoid bulkiness where layers of applique overlap (where a petal and stem come together, for example), stitch only the top layer.

No mess

* Wrap a couple of pieces of double faced tape around an empty thread spool and you'll be able to get rid of thread clippings or ravelings that would otherwise stick to your fingers while sewing.

Threads

* Use threads labeled "quilting" for quilts; they are stronger than regular sewing threads.
* Run threads over a piece of beeswax as you sew. It strengthens the threads and makes it easier to pull through the layers of fabric.
* Or, dip the quilting threads into melted paraffin. Remove them and let cool. The thread will slide through the fabric.

Thread tension

* Reduce the tension of the top thread -- while letting the bobbin tension remain constant, and your quilt or applique will have a smooth rounded satin stitch on top.

This and that

* If you don't like thimbles, but want to prevent pricked fingers, wrap your fingers with plastic bandages when quilting.

* Or, use a rubber finger protector designed for filing (available at office supply stores).
* Press the seam of quilted pieces to one side, instead of open, and the seam will be stronger.

Storage of quilts

* The best place to store a quilt may be on your bed because folding and storing it improperly weakens the fibers.

Rolling a quilt is best

* Find a wooden pole or cardboard mailing tube at least 5" longer than the length of the quilt. Cover the roll with plastic wrap or brown paper. Loosely roll the quilt on the tube and hang from a curtain rod or other brackets in a dark, well-ventilated room. Avoid temperature extremes. Cover with a loose plastic sheet.
* Or, roll the quilt in a clean sheet and pack away.

Folding methods

* If rolling is impractical and you must fold, remember that creases are the enemy. Pad the folds with sheets of tissue paper. Put the quilt in a roomy plastic bag. Leave the bag open.

* Unless the quilt is of wool. In that case, add a cup of moth flakes and seal the bag.
* Refold any stored quilt several times a year.

The Best of Hints for
SEWING
BY HAND

A stitch in time...

Tools of the trade
* Rusty needles can be smoothed by rubbing with a steel wool or soap filled pad.
* Run a dull pin or needle through your hair before using and your hair's natural oils will lubricate the pin.
* Or, keep needles lubricated by stabbing them into a bar of soap before use.

Zipper magic
* Stuck zippers will run smoothly if you take a candle and rub it over the teeth of the zipper.

This one's a snap!
* Use a candle to lubricate a snap that's difficult to unfasten.

Erase your problems
* Use a pencil eraser to remove loose threads from a ripped-out seam.

Tricks for threading a needle
* Spray your finger with spray starch; pinch the thread. The starch will stiffen the thread.
* Or, use hair spray.
* And, place a white card behind the needle -- it will help you see the eye better.

Thread madness
* Always thread your needle before you cut the thread from the spool. Thread has a twist that will cause it to tangle if you thread the wrong end.
* Select thread a shade darker than the fabric you're sewing; thread appears lighter on the fabric than it does on the spool.
* To store your thread spools, take an empty cigar box, glue golf tees to the inside bottom on the box. When the glue is dry, slip the spools over the tees.

A cure for dull scissors

* Scissors can be sharpened by cutting through a fine grade of sandpaper.
* Or, try to "cut" the neck of a wine bottle l5-20 times; the slipping will sharpen them.
* If the scissors are new and too stiff to close easily, lubricate the blades by carefully rubbing the inside of the blades with your finger -- your natural oils do the trick.

Separate those tiny beads

* Sift beads from sequins by pouring them into a colander. The beads will fall through leaving the sequins in the top.

Here are some snappy ideas

* To get snap fasteners in position, sew one half in position. Put chalk on its tip. Place the other side of the garment in position; press down. The chalk will leave a mark where you'll want to sew your second snap half.
* If you cover snap fasteners with transparent tape before you sew, they won't slip out of place. After sewing, remove the tape.

Cutting on the bias

* When you need to cut a bias strip from fabric, place a strip of masking tape on the fabric (on the bias) cut on both sides of the tape, remove tape.

An emergency kit

* An empty pill bottle will hold a thimble, a bobbin with thread, a needle or two, pins, and a safety pin -- all for quick repairs when traveling.

Button, button, who's got the button?

* Coat the bottom of metal buttons with clear nail polish before you sew them on. This will prevent rust marks when washing.
* When sewing on buttons, make the thread stronger by running it through beeswax (available in the notions' department).
* You can reinforce children's jacket buttons, or others to come under heavy strain. On the inside of the garment, directly under the jacket button, place a small felt button. Sew all buttons and layers together.
* Sew buttons in place with a straight pin laid across the top. Remove the pin after sewing. This slightly looser sewing makes a thread shank and provides "give."

No knots

* You can eliminate the knot when sewing on a button. Double the thread, thread the needle with the two ends. Put the needle through the fabric, leaving the uncut loop on the wrong side. Put the needle through the fabric again, this time through the loop. Pull taut; complete sewing as usual.

Clipped corners

* To prevent cutting too far when you have to clip into a corner before turning a seam, pin a straight pin on the seam line.

For an accurate hemline

* Allow garments to hang 24 hours when finished, before hemming. This gives the fabric a chance to settle before you measure and hem.

Measuring the hemline

* The best way to mark a hem length is to have a friend measure, while you are wearing the garment, up from the floor with a yardstick.
* Lay the garment on a table or other flat surface and be certain the hem is straight. If it is curved, distribute the fullness evenly.
* Always pin at right angles to the hem. Pinning either at a slant or parallel to the hem may cause the hem to twist.

You don't need a hem gauge

* To measure your hem depth use a 3" x 5" card, a postcard from a magazine, or other lightweight cardboard. Cut a notch at the proper depth, and pin.
* Or, cut a piece of cardboard the depth of your hem. Slide it along in your hem as you sew.
* To reduce the bulk in a hem at a seam, mark hem as usual. Cut away 1/2" of the 5/8" seam allowance in the upturned hem portion only. Sew as usual.

Skirt lining simplified

* Easy! Cut the lining using the skirt pattern. Assemble the pieces making darts and side seams. Attach it to the skirt only at the waistband; sew it into the waistline seam. Hem it separately, 3/4" shorter than the skirt.
* Easier! Buy a close fitting half slip of a non-stretchy fabric (such as taffeta) and attach it to your skirt's waistband.

* Easiest! Make it a point to wear a taffeta slip with knit or stretchy clothes.

Sewing braided rugs
* Use fishing line. It wears longer than carpet twine.

No more pulled out drawstrings
* You can keep them in sweatshirts and other garments. Pull both ends of the drawstring out even. Sew a line of stitches across the casing at the middle back of the garment.

Preventing bathroom clutter
* If you sew a couple of snaps on the ends of a handtowel and snap the towel around the towel bar, your children's towels will no longer end up on the floor.

Pincushions
* Save hair for stuffing pincushions. The natural oils will prevent rust.
* Or, stuff a pincushion will shavings from your pencil sharpener. The graphite prevents rust.
* Or, make a "doughnut." Take a pair of old pantyhouse. Cut the legs, discard the panty. Put one leg inside the other. Starting from the top, roll to the toe. Your "doughnut" will hold your pins.

The tiniest pincushion
* Stick a filter from a filtertip cigarette in the hole of your spool of thread and you'll have the world's tiniest pincushion.

Putting scraps to use
* Glue felt scraps on the rough bottom of vases and no more furniture scratches.
* Left-over fabric pieces can be used to cover photo picture frames.
* And, as mats for photos.
* Dress up plain metal bookends with remnants. Cut 2 pieces of fabric for each bookend. Cut 3/4" larger all around then the bookend's upright section. Keeping right sides together, sew a 5/8" seam on three sides (leaving the bottom open). Clip corners, turn right side out. Slip onto bookend. Voila!

The Best of Hints for
SEWING
BY MACHINE

It's "Oh, sew easy!"

Using patterns
* Frequently used pattern pieces can be cut out of non-woven interfacing and then can be written on, or washed, without tearing.
* Iron pattern pieces you will use so they will lay flat.
* Prevent patterns from wearing out along marked darts, etc. by putting transparent tape along those lines. You'll still be able to see through the reinforced lines.

Easier than pinning patterns
* Is to weight them down with fishing weights.
* Or, silverware.

If you can't find your tracing wheel
* You can use the tines of a fork with dressmaker's carbon to mark the outlines of darts, etc.

Easy pattern reference
* Cut pattern envelopes open and tape onto a manila envelope. You will be able to see all the information at one time, and when your project is completed, it will be much easier to fit the pattern back into the envelope, and file.

Cutting pile fabrics
* When you are working with very bulky or slippery fabrics, cut off the pattern margins before placing them on the fabric because it will be easier to cut along the edge of the tissue.
* Deep pile and fake furs will be more easily cut if you use a razor blade. Cut only the backing, and from the wrong side, so the pile is not cut (protect your work surface).

The machine
* Sharpen dull needles by stitching through a piece of sandpaper.
* A bent needle can break during sewing, fly up and hit you. Don't sew "just one more seam," it could be dangerous.

Runaway foot pedal?

* Keep a machine foot pedal from slipping on bare floors by wrapping a couple of wide rubber bands around it.

Cleaning your sewing machine

* Use sewing machine oil on a cotton swab to get at hard to reach areas of your sewing machine.
* After oiling your sewing machine, stitch through a blotter. Excess oil will be removed and your fabrics will not be stained.
* Or, stitch through a double thickness of paper toweling.
* Clean lint from your machine by spraying with a lint removing aerosal (available at photo supply stores).

Add seam allowance quidelines

* If your machine does not have guidelines, draw your own. Mark a line 5/8" (the standard seam allowance) to the right and left of the needle. You can use a marking pen, fingernail polish, or adhesive tape.

Avoid skipped stitches

* On knit and stretch fabrics use a ball point needle in your machine -- it's rounded, not sharp.
* In addition, launder the fabric to remove any excess sticky chemical residue which may eventually cause the needle to skip.
* And, occasionally wipe the needle with lighter fluid to remove any residue.

Stitching darts

* Always stitch darts from the wide end to the point. Tie off the threads ends with a square knot.

Difficult fabrics

* Lace can be prevented from catching in the feed dog if you place strips of tissue paper between the lace and the machine. Tear the paper away when the stitching is completed.
* Tissue paper is also useful under nylon and other slippery fabrics.

Working with nylon net

* Regular pins will slip out of nylon net -- use fine hairpins to hold seams together.

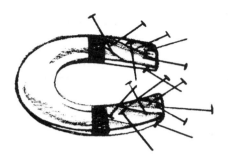

Repair holes in sheets

* Again, using a sheet of thin paper under the hole, sew back and forth covering the hole with stitches. When you next wash the sheet, the paper will disintergrate.

Recovering spilled pins

* Keep a small magnet at the machine for picking up spilled steel pins.

Handling elastic -- it's a snap!

* Cut elastic l/2'' less than the wrist measurement, cut it 4'' less than the waist measurement.
* Elastic bands can be fed into waist, leg, or arm casings easily by using a safety pin. Fasten the pin to one end of the elastic, feed it into the casing, push through to the far end, hold both ends, stitch together.
* Or, when replacing old elastic with new, do it this way. Pin one end of the new elastic to one end of the old elastic. Pull the old out by its other end, replacing it with the new.

With leather

* When sewing with leather, use paper clips to hold the edges together.
* Never backstitch -- it can cut the leather.
* Spread a thin line of rubber cement over the stitches on the underside of the seam allowance. Fingerpress the seam allowance against the garment.

A buttonhole sampler

* Next time you have to make a buttonhole you will have a guide if you have made a buttonhole sampler. With your button hole attachment, make all the various sizes possible. Label each by size. When you make a garment, check to see which size buttonhole you will need for the buttons.

Notions

* Prevent headaches by preshrinking zippers. Immerse the zipper in hot water for a few minutes, allow to dry. Repeat, press before using.
* Preshink all notions -- laces, trims, tapes, and bindings not labeled "preshrunk."

No basting

* Instead of basting in zippers, tape them in place for sewing with adhesive tape. When finished sewing, pull away the tape.

Easy cording

* Rather than cutting fabric on the bias, use bias tape, which you wrap around cording, to put the edging on handmade pillows.

A decorative thread holder

* Buy a small bread board with a handle. Evenly space 24 headless nails or wood screws -- four across, six down. Put cup hooks along the bottom for hanging scissors, tape measures, etc. Hang and enjoy.

Inventory control

* Keep track of yardage with inventory control! On each storage box, in a file box, or on a bulletin board, keep a small swatch of each stored fabric. Write the approximate yardage on the scrap with a felt tip pen -- then you'll see at a glance what you have on hand.

You can be organized

* Save empty pill bottles and 35mm film cans for storage of sewing needles, snaps, and matched sets of buttons.

A snake for stopping drafts

* Measure the door's width, add l2". Cut a piece of fabric 6" wide. With right sides together, sew 1" seams across one end and along the side. Turn right side out. Stuff with kitty litter. Slipstitch end closed.

A jacket lining

* Use a designer scarf for a colorful, unusual jacket lining.

Roll-up organizers

* Use scraps for roll-up organizers of knitting needles, silverware, camping pots and pans, sewing accessories, etc.

A "tooth fairy" pocket

* Sew a pocket on a child's pillowcase. Make it small enough to hold the lost tooth, large enough for the tooth fairy's coin.

Pet's safety collar

* Stitch reflective tape (available at variety stores) to your pet's collar for safety after dark.

An eyeglass case

* Take a pot holder, fold in half, sew across one end and up the side, for a quick, inexpensive, original, and colorful eyeglass case.

The Best of Hints for

ODDS
'N
ENDS

A little of this 'n a little of that!

Tools of the trade

* Run thread over beeswax or paraffin. It strengthens the thread and also makes it easier to pull through thick material.
* Don't ever cut paper with your sewing scissors; it dulls the edges.
* Sharpen dull scissors by cutting through fine sandpaper several times.

Needles and pins

* With sewing needles the smaller the number, the larger the needle.
* Use sharp fine needles for pinning delicate fabrics that could be damaged by regular pins.

Selecting needles

* Betweens: A sharp needle, usually used for quilting.
* Bodkins: A large eyed needle, usually used for threading cord, ribbon, or elastic.
* Chenilles: A sharp needle, larger than the crewel needle, used with thick threads on stitchery.
* Crewels: A sharp, medium length needle, usually used for stitchery.
* Sharps: A sharp, short needle, for general sewing.
* Tapestry: A medium to larger needle, blunt, that is used for counted thread work and needlepoint.

Remove straight pins

* Don't leave straight pins in fabrics you're storing away. They may rust or leave enlarged holes.

Thread tapestry needles easily

* Fold 1" of your yarn over the needle, pull taut. Pinch this fold with thumb and forefinger. Slip off needle, push pinched fold through needle.
* Or, you can use a paper strip. Cut the strip 1/4" wide, 2" long. Fold the strip in half crosswise. Insert yarn. Push folded paper through needle eye.

Avoid interrupting your work

* When you are working with many different colors, thread the various colors on different needles before you start.

Measure twice, cut once!

* Cloth tape measures may stretch with use. Check them occasionally for accuracy.
* Start measurements on a yardstick or ruler with the 1" mark, and when you're done, subtract 1". This advice because the measure at the end is often worn or off-register.

Did you know?

* A dollar bill is 1/16" less than 6".

Learn your measurements

* If you learn the distance between your outstretched thumb and forefinger, your outstretched thumb and little finger, and so forth, you will have a built in ruler that will come in handy when you don't have a tape measure.

Cleanliness is....

* Carrying a few packages of foil-wrapped soaped towels in your needlework bag. You will have clean hands to work with no matter where you go.
* Avoiding cleaning problems by wearing an apron, or a lap cloth, and washing your hands before you pick up your needlework.

Dye transfer

* Check your needlework occasionally to be certain that the dye in your clothing is not rubbing off on your fabric as you work.

Keep a clean copy

* Place your needlework instructions in a plastic sleeve (available where binder notebooks are found).

Notebook for memories

* Keep a notebook of all the needlecraft projects you've completed. Jot down a brief description including the size, who it was for, when you finished it. Attach a swatch of fabric, a bit of yarn, several threads. Add a photo if you have one. You'll be amazed at all you have accomplished -- and you may otherwise forget about many of the projects you've given as gifts.

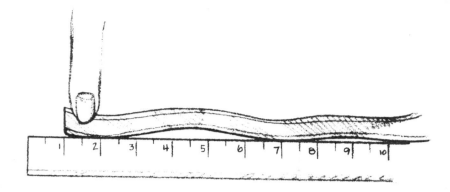

Don't tire your eyes!

* Your eyes need a rest. Stop your close work occasionally and focus on a point across the room or across the street.
* When starting a needlecraft project, remember that your eye muscles need time to adjust. Work for a short time, then resume your normal activities. Each day as you come back to the needlecraft you can work a little longer.

Throw some light on the subject

* Use a soft-light lightbulb or natural light when you work. Be sure that the light comes over your shoulder and onto your work -- not into your eyes.
* Use a magnifying glass when doing close work, such as petit point. Don't damage your eyesight.

Need some exercise?

* Get the circulation going; get the cramps out of your fingers. With your arms at your sides, elbows slightly bent, let your fingers come up, then down, with a snapping motion at the wrist.
* Or, hold your arms out in front of you and pretend you're playing scales on the piano.

"Oh, oh!"

* Whenever possible on women's sweaters and blouses, make the buttonholes run horizontally and they won't pop open!

Dress head first

* Always put skirts and dresses on over your head. Stepping into a skirt often breaks the zipper, strains the fabric, and if your heel catches -- pulls out the hem.

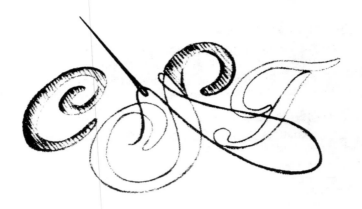

Another bottle of polish
* A thin coat of clear fingernail polish can be applied to the raw edges of cottons that fray (denim, flannel, etc.) to prevent fraying when washing.

"Holes" barred
* Rubber protectors sold for knitting needles are also good on scissor points.
* Or, use a cork. This will protect your needle points and your needlework bag.

No glue mess
* If you cut a fingertip from an old pair of rubber gloves, you can use it to spread the glue.

How to clean your iron
* Clean the soleplate of your iron by using your warm iron on salt you have sprinkled on brown paper. Note: don't try this on teflon-coated surfaces.
* Wax the bottom of your iron by running the warm iron over waxpaper.

Monograms
* When monograms are all the same size, they are placed in this order: first, maiden, married name.
* When the center monogram is largest, the initials are placed in this order: (for the hope chest) first, surname, middle name; (after marriage) first, married surname, maiden surname.

Don't hide it away!

* An heirloom hanky or piece of lace can be displayed, instead of hidden away. Sandwich it between two pieces of glass; mount in an aluminum channeled frame. Hang it in the window -- but not in the direct sun.

A tailored bed ruffle

* Your mattress and bedsprings sit on the floor -- how to hide the spring ticking? Put a fitted sheet which matches or contrasts with your bedspread upside down on the box springs.

Recipe for rose pomander

* Gather roses and a few leaves in the morning. Spread the petals on newspaper, and sprinkle them with salt. Turn daily. When thoroughly dry, place them in a large container. Add I tablespoon of glycerin (from drugstore) per quart of petals. Stir to coat. You may add some of your favorite perfume for fragrance, soon the roses will supply their own.

Recipe for pomander ball

* Select thick-skinned oranges, lemons, or limes. Stick straight pins through whole cloves and into the fruit. Completely cover the surface of the fruit. Roll in a mixture of cinnamon and orris root (from drugstore). Tie a ribbon around the fruit, hang it in a closet several weeks to become hard and fragrant.

How to make a "chatelaine"

* A very useful item for keeping tabs on your needles, pins, scissors, and thimble. Wear it around your neck as professional dressmakers do. Cut a 1" wide piece of grosgrain ribbon approximately 65" long. Fold one end up and stitch to form a small pocket for your thimble and a tiny pincushion. Tie your scissors with the other end. Mark the ribbon at 1" intervals and you will have a tape measure.

The Best of Hints for
TRANSFERS & DESIGNS

Get 'em while they're hot!

Iron-on transfers
* Work best on light or medium color fabrics with little texture. Consider the colors of the transfer before you buy the fabric (a blue transfer won't show well on a blue fabric).

Preparation
* Cut off unwanted words, lines, and captions before you start to iron-on the transfer.

Applying the transfer
* Match the setting of the iron to the material being used (i.e. wool, cotton, synthetic). Preheat the iron 5 minutes, never use steam.
* Use a test transfer on a scrap of your material to count how many seconds of heat are required.
* Use the heated iron to smooth the fabric, then pin pattern ink side down.
* Do not slide the iron -- lift from place to place.
* Use the shortest transfer time needed -- you'll get more repeats from the transfer.

Save your transfers
* Good quality transfers can be used up to 5 times on some fabrics.

Protect delicate fabrics
* Place tissue paper, brown paper, or a pressing cloth over transfer designs.
* To apply transfers to a stretchy fabric (like a t-shirt), insert a piece of cardboard between the fabric and the ironing board so you'll have a smooth, firm surface.

A culprit
* Sometimes iron-on transfers won't adhere properly. It may be that your fabric has so much sizing that it won't accept the transfer. If you suspect that may be the problem, wash the fabric.

Iron-on transfers on needlepoint!

* You can apply iron-on transfers to needlepoint canvas. You will find a wide selection of patterns to choose from, and save a lot of time applying the design.

Colored cross stitch transfers!

* There are now cross stitch transfers on the market that indicate the color to be worked. No need to count threads, no need to refer to a key.

Transfers on wood

* You can apply transfer patterns to wood for tole and wood-burning work.

Steps for applying transfers to wood

* Use a light colored wood such as bass wood.
* Heat the iron to the cotton setting.
* Place the transfer face down on the wood's surface.
* Place a cover sheet (typing paper or brown paper will do) over the transfer and the wood.
* It will take 20 to 100 seconds for the transfer process to be completed. Carefully check the progress of the transfer, don't let the transfer shift.
* To prevent sticking, remove transfer while still hot.
* Apply a thin coat of sealer before and after tracing the design so the wood's sap will not seep out.

Transfer pencils

* With transfer pencils you can create your own transfer designs.
* Use a hard-leaded pencil so you will have a fine-lined transfer. Inexpensive wax transfer pencils make a thick line that tends to smudge and smear.
* Use transfer pencils on light to medium colored fabrics.

Be careful of pin marks

* When you pin carbon into place the needle holes will leave marks on the fabric -- so be careful where you pin.

Tracing

* Use a medium or sharp pencil to trace accurately and clearly. A soft lead should not be used for regular tracing because it smudges.

* A glass topped table is marvelous for tracing patterns. Just set a lamp on the floor and let the light illuminate your work.
* Or, try the traditional approach of holding your drawing up against a well-lit window.

Pricking

* Position the design on your fabric. Pin in place. Prick with a pin. Rub ponce (a fine powder) over the holes. Remove pattern, blow off excess powder. Connect dots with pencil.
* Use your sewing machine for pricking. Remove the machine threads; stitch along the lines of the design.

Other methods

* Velvets, heavy woolens, and other fabrics that won't accept carbon paper need another method. Trace your design onto tissue paper. Position the paper; baste the outline and lines of design with small stitches made with a contrasting thread. Remove the tissue paper. Work your design.
* Stretchy t-shirts can be worked by basting a piece of tissue or non-stretchy sheer fabric to the back. Embroider the design as usual. Cut away excess tissue or cloth, leave it in the design area.

Enlarging

* Study the scale of your pattern. Draw the number of squares indicated. If each square (as is usual) is one square is equal to l", draw your lines l" apart vertically and horizontally. In each of your new squares, draw what is shown in the corresponding pattern's square. When finished, doublecheck.

A novel approach

* Use your typewriter for making graph paper for enlarging. Pica has 10 spaces per inch, elite 12 per inch. Set tab stops and across the page you go! 6 vertical lines makes an inch. Complete your dot pattern, connect dots, and draw your design.

Money and time savers

* Save the paper backing from contact paper -- it's marked with l" squares which you can use next time you want graph paper.
* Draw your squares on lightweight paper, cover with waxed paper. Draw the design. When you remove the waxed paper, you will have your pattern, yet the original graph will be unmarked and can be used again.

To blow up designs
* Take your design to a photocopier and have her enlarge or reduce your pattern to the size you want.

Use your projector
* Take a slide picture of the design you want. Project the slide onto a wall, moving the projector closer or farther away to change to size of the projected image. Tape a sheet of paper or fabric on the wall. Draw the pattern using a felt tip pen.

The pantograph
* If you do a lot of reducing or enlarging of patterns, you might consider a pantograph. It is a mechanical device (available at art supply stores) that makes quick work of copying drawings.

The accuracy of color
* Check the color of the yarn you are about to buy outdoors or by a window. Artificial lights often distort color.

The color wheel
* "Monochromatic" means using several values of one color.
* "Related" or "analogous" colors are those that are close on the color wheel -- being neighbors, they are harmonious.
* "Complementary" colors are those opposite each other on the color wheel. The colors may be powerful, and tricky as they compete. Proceed with caution, perhaps using one as an accent.

Color terms

* Hue refers to the color (red, blue, orange, etc.); to change the hue, you add another color.
* 'Value" indicates the relation of the color to white and black. When you add white or black to a color, you change to a lighter or darker value. When we talk about a light blue or a dark blue, we are discussing value.
* 'Intensity" refers to color strength or saturation. To change the intensity of a color, you add gray. When we call colors "brilliant" or "dull", we are refering to the intensity.

Colors and our emotions

* Colors affect our emotions and express traditional ideas. Reds, oranges, and yellows are "advancing" or warm -- think of fire, the sun, light. Blues, blue-greens, and blue-violets are "retreating" or cool -- think of the sky, the sea. White symbolizes innocence, light, joy. Black symbolizes the power of darkness, solidity, and restful quiet.

The range of colors in yarns

* Synthetics yarns are available in a wider range of colors than natural yarns -- particularly in the bright colors.
* Natural yarns are available in a wider range of muted colors than are synthetic yarns.

To fade or not to fade

* Vat dyed fabrics are less likely to fade than fabrics that are printed.
* Dark colored fabrics are more likely to fade than light colored fabrics.
* When you're selecting materials for a project, remember that dyed burlap tends to fade quickly. You might want to reserve its use for stitcheries that will be covered entirely with yarn.

Easy appliques

* Use transfers to make appliques and patches. Apply the transfer as usual, leaving at least 2" around the pattern while working. When applique is completed, stitch around the design. Clip as needed, trim to 1/4". Turn raw edges under; press. Slipstitch into place.

Add a dimensional effect

* Insert a small piece of batting between the appliqued piece and the background fabric before stitching.

With punch embroidery

* You can even more easily turn transfers into appliques. Punch your design. Coat the back of the fabric with washable fabric glue, let dry, then trim right up to the edge of the design.

Ornaments

* Turn extra transfer patterns into Christmas (or other) ornaments. Color a suitable pattern. Glue to lightweight cardboard; allow to dry. Cut out outline. Glue matching pattern to back, or a solid color. Color cut edges with felt tip pen. Poke a hole for string, hang.

Projects to make with transfers

* Make toys, small pillows, sachets, pin holders, ornaments. Transfer the design onto one side of a fabric piece, the wrong side of another. Cut out the pieces. Placing right sides together, stitch leaving room to turn. Turn, stuff, and then slipstitch closed.
* Decorative flowers can be made from scraps of fabric cut into flower shapes using suitable transfer patterns. Transfer, cut, sew, stuff, insert a wire "stem," and enjoy!

Personalize with transfers

* Use monogram or alphabet transfers to create wedding, graduation, and baby samplers.
* Use transfers to personalize a needlecraft gift with birthsign, flower of the month, or occupation.

For children

* Use transfers to make children's story boards using felt for the characters and board.
* Apply transfers directly onto the walls of the nursery and then paint in the colors.

Try outlining

* Trace the outline of a design from a transfer book, magazine, or coloring book. Pin the design in place. Zigzag stitch around the design edges and the detail lines. Tear away the paper, leaving the design intact.

You can find design ideas many places

* Textiles: fashion and upholstery fabrics, and linens.
* Papers: children's coloring books, magazines, greeting cards, wrapping papers, wallpaper sample books, and art prints.
* Nature: leaves, flowers, birds, animals, and rocks.

The Best of Hints for
FINISHING TOUCHES

Don't leave it hanging!

A little vise
* To hold thin frames together while glue sets, use a screw-type earring.

Framing your work
* If you can't find the right size frame for your stitchery, make your own. Many hobby, art supply, or lumber dealers sell frame kits that are easy to assemble.
* If your frame is too large, cut a mat to fit. If you don't want the paper mat to show, you can cover it with a fabric that matches or contrasts with your needlework.

Defeat the enemies
* Hang needlework away from strong light and heat sources -- sunlight, fluorescent lights, heat vents. Heat and strong lights will fade colors and weaken textiles.

Mounting your work
* When mounting needlework as a framed picture, choose a frame with an opening slightly smaller than your completed piece. Center the work on a piece of cardboard 1/8" smaller, each dimension, than the inside frame opening. Turn the edges of the fabric to the back. Tape with masking tape. Place in frame. Fasten in place with small rustproof nails. Cover the back entirely with brown paper. Wire for hanging; hang in place. Step back and admire!

To mount on hardboard
* Cut the work with at least 3" all around for turning. Fix the edges so they won't unravel. Fold the edges around the board -- carefully centering your design. Miter and fold the corners; secure with tape. Thread a darning needle with carpet or other heavy thread. Knot. Starting at the top center, go to the bottom center. Continue to "lace" your way to the corner. Return to the center top; this time "lace" to the opposite corner. Start a new thread, and do the sides in the same manner -- beginning with their centers.

Added insight

* To avoid the "show through" of the stretcher frame on which you are mounting your needlework, pad the frame. Cover the frame with muslin or sheeting, stretched tightly. You will also achieve a nice padded effect.

How to stain picture frames

* Unfinished frames can be stained with shoe polish or wax. Experiment on the back of the frame.

Matting

* Use a mat that is acid-free (available at art supply stores) when matting valuable art work or stitchery. Acid-pulp papers may discolor and damage your work.

Hang heavy frames to stay

* It's important to hang heavy frames or projects securely. Try to hang from a wall stud. Use a magnetic stud finder (inexpensive, available at the hardware store) to locate nails in the studs. Most homes have studs placed 16" apart.

Don't crack the plaster!

* When hanging craft projects on the wall, protect the wall. Crisscross two short pieces of cellophane tape over the point where you want to drive the nail. This reduces cracking of the plaster.

Cutting foam rubber

* An electric knife (from your kitchen) makes it easy to cut foam rubber to size.

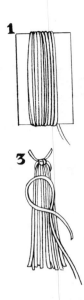
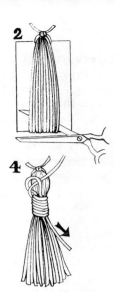

How to make a tassel

* Wind yarn around a piece of cardboard the length you want the finished tassel. (The more times you wind, the thicker the tassel). Cut a length of yarn, slip under one end of strands on cardboard and tie securely. Cut strands at opposite end. Cut a piece of yarn (15″ or more). Fold a loop, place it against tassel. Keeping a 3″ tail, begin winding 1/3 the distance from the secured end of tassel. Thread end through the loop, pull tail end until loop disappears under wrapping. Shape end of tassel.

Fashioning a pompon

* Cut two cardboard disks desired size of pompon. Cut hole in center of each (doughnut fashion). Thread a blunt needle with two strands of yarn. Place disks together; wrap with yarn until covered, working thru holes. Cut all strands at outside edge. Wind a strand of yarn between the disks several times, tightly. Knot, leaving ends for attaching pompon. Remove disks. Fluff yarn into shape.
* Use metal washers for making pompons. No more cutting cardboard doughnuts.

A fringe benefit

* To make fringe cut strands to suggested length. Fold strand in half. With crochet hook draw folded end partly through edge to wrong side of work. Put loose ends through folded end. Pull tight.

How to make a fabric fringe

* Cut the edge to be fringed along the grainline. Measure up the distance you want for fringe depth. With pin find the crosswise thread, and pull. This is your guideline -- the top of your fringe. Sew close stitches (16-20 per inch by machine) along this line. Unravel surplus threads, forming fringe.

All about buttons

* Metal and other buttons with sharp edges on the shank will cut your thread or yarn. Coat the edges with clear fingernail polish and let dry. Sew in place.
* Or, sew them on with carpet thread.
* Or, dental floss.
* Attach buttons to coats with elastic cord. The "give" will make the button fasten easily, but not strain the fastening.

Quick sewing

* Buttons will go on faster if you fold the thread, making 4 strands, and sew.

Remember this for Thanksgiving dinner!

* Buttons sewn on with elastic thread at the waistband will "give" when you gain a bit of weight.

Our old friend

* Preserve the metal finish on buttons, belt buckles, and other metal trims with a coating of clear fingernail polish.

Soft stuffings for pillows

* Use the lint from your dryer for filling small items -- Christmas ornaments, pin cushions, and so forth. It's clean and it's free.
* Use those old pantyhose. Wash, cut into small pieces (discard the panty section), and stuff into pillows, children's toys and animals. It's washable and lightweight.
* Or, use clothes dryer softener sheets.

Firm stuffings

* Use vermiculite or cat litter where you want weight to your stuffing -- in floor pillows, for example. Don't use where it will get wet.
* You can also use sand or sawdust when you want weight. It's firm and it's often free. Don't let it get wet!

The Best of Hints for
STAINS, REPAIRS & CLEANING

Take the pain out of your stain!

Easing a zipper
* If the fabric is a light color, rub the zipper with a light colored candle.
* If the fabric is a dark color, lubricate the zipper by rubbing the teeth with a lead pencil.

Darning
* When you can't find your wooden darning egg, use a dry ornamental gourd.

Bring out the white vinegar
* To get rid of the creases caused by a lowered hemline, brush on some white vinegar applied with a small paint brush (pretest colorfastness in an inconspicuous area of garment).
* To get rid of shiny areas on the back of skirts and slacks (again, pretest).
* And, to make permanent creases use a presscloth dampened with 3 parts water to 1 part vinegar on the line you wish to set.

Blue jeans blues?
* Get rid of that tell-tale white line on lengthened blue jeans -- use a permanent ink marking pen, and color in the line.
* Or, paint the white line with liquid embroidery. It is available in many, many colors.
* Wash a pair of new jeans with a pair of old jeans and the excess dye will come out of the new ones and color the old ones.

Jeans and patches
* After your children have worn their jeans a couple of times, you will be able to see where the pants' knees will wear. Iron, or sew, large patches on the inside of the pants and the knees won't get baggy or wear out as fast.
* A piece of iron-on tape on the inside bottom of a cuff will keep it from rolling up. The tape will also prevent the cuff from wearing at the heel.

Thrifty tip

* Before you throw out old clothing, check for useful notions -
  - zipper, buttons, and pockets.

Fuzz balls?

* Pills, or fuzz balls, on the collars of shirts or on the body of
  machine-knit garments can be removed. Shave them off
  carefully with a dry razor.

Ironing

* Small areas of napped fabrics (corduroy, velvet, etc.) can be
  pressed without being crushed. Set a stiff clothesbrush, tufts
  up, on a flat surface. Place your fabric right side down on the
  brush. Using a pressing cloth, press your fabric gently (on the
  wrong side) with a steam iron.
* When pressing the hem of bonded knits, place a moist press
  cloth over the lower half of the hem. Press, avoiding weight on
  the iron -- which might cause an embossed line on the garment.

Revitalizing old down or feather pillows

* First check for, and repair, any breaks or tears in your pillow.
  Place the pillow in your clothes dryer with a heavy damp
  towel. Tumble at a cool setting for 20 minutes.

General rules on stains

* Absord excess liquid with a clean cloth or white paper towel.
  Touch the liquid, not the fabric. Avoid forcing stains into the
  fabric.
* Before you start any cleaning procedure, including water, test
  to be sure you won't be harming the dye or fabric.
* Test colorfastness in an inconspicuous spot such as the inside
  of a pocket, hem, seam, or shirttail.

Avoid the vapors!

* Whenever using a solvent for cleaning be sure to use proper
  ventilation.
* And, be certain to let any solvents dry before coming in contact with your skin.

Be careful with bleach

* Never use full strength, undiluted bleach -- it eats holes in
  fabrics. The proper dilution is 1 part bleach to 4 parts water.

Categories of stains

* Water based stains (on washable fabrics) such as tea, coffee, fruit juice, and alcohol -- soak in cold water immediately.
* Oil, wax, and grease stains -- dust with talcum powder, they will require cleaning solvents.
* Chemical substances such as paints, lacquers, and glues -- should be treated by a professional dry cleaner.

Sponging stains

* Use a cloth or small sponge. Work on an inverted glass pie plate or some other surface that will not be stained. Work from the outside of the stain to the inside, keeping the wetted area as small as possible. Make the outside edges irregular so that there will not be a discernable line when the fabric is dry. Change the sponging pad, and any absorbent cloth underneath, whenever any of the stain is picked up (to prevent reapplying the stain). Work gently, don't rub.
* You can use an embroidery hoop for holding the stained area taut while you work on it.

To work stains by tamping

* Use a small clean brush. "Tamp" the cleaning solution into the fabric by using the brush as you would a small tack hammer. Work gently to avoid damaging fibers.

Use a spoon

* Use a stainless steel spoon. Turn in on its side and with the bowl of the spoon make gentle scraping motions as you work in the cleaning solution.

Special stains (test first)

* If you prick your finger and get a drop of blood on your needlework, all is not lost. If the fabric is washable, immediately treat it to a bath of lukewarm salty water followed by a wash of lukewarm soapy water.
* Or, use your own saliva.
* Apply unseasoned meat tenderizer to old blood stains. Add water to make a paste, let set 30 minutes. Wash.
* The smell and stain of sour milk can often be eliminated by wiping the area with a cloth moistened with white vinegar and water.

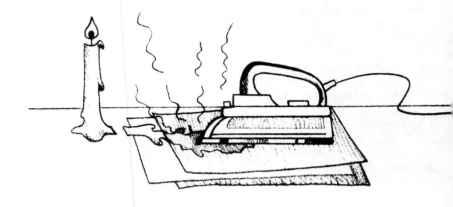

To the freezer!
* Chewing gum, and the residue of adhesive tape, can be removed by putting the garment in a plastic bag and into the freezer.
* Or, hold an ice cube against the sticky substance, then scrape with a spoon.

Ink spots
* Ballpoint ink can often be removed by spraying with hairspray before washing.

Carbon paper
* Work a paste made of granular dishwashing soap and water into the stain. Rinse.
* If the stain persists, put a few drops of ammonia on the stain, repeat the detergent treatment.

Road tar
* Tar should be rubbed with kerosene until removed; then wash the garment.

Candlewax
* Removed by placing the stained area between two pieces of brown paper. Press with an iron until it's absorbed.

Food stains

* Club soda is a good spot remover. Good thing to remember when eating out.
* Club soda can also remove grease from suede. After treatment, brush the nap back in place.

Red wine spilled?

* Try sprinkling the spot liberally with salt. Flush with cold water, rub out the stain.
* Alcohol should be removed or eventually a stain will appear. Treat with cold water to which a few drops of glycerine have been added. Rinse with white vinegar and water.

If all else fails...

* Sometimes you can hide a stain with a strategically placed pocket.
* Or, an embroidered design.
* Or, an applique.
* Or, by adding a decorative panel.
* Or, with a decorative ruffle.

Washing

* Don't overload your washer. Clothes will come out as dirty as when they went in -- and dirt is abrasive, it causes excess wear on your clothes.
* Don't wash clothes too long. Detergents only hold dirt in suspension for so long.

Washing a quilt with cotton batting

* Mend any tears before washing. Fill a large basin or tub with warm water, use a mild soap. Drop the quilt into the water and agitate it with your hands. Rinse several times. Do not wring! Squeeze out excess water. Hang from a clothesline, preferably draped over two lines. Distribute the weight evenly; never hang from one end!

With polyester batting

* Hand or machine wash with the gentle cycle. Rinse thoroughly (repeating machine cycles if necessary). Fluff dry with low-heat. If in doubt about the machine, stick with hand-washing.

To the cleaners

* If you send your quilt to the cleaners, be sure to give it plenty of time to air dry at home before you store or use it -- to clear out any cleaning solvent odors.

Repairing snags

* You can quickly pull snags to the back of "store-bought" clothing using a sewing needle threader. Just push the threader through from the inside of the garment, catch the snag, and pull it through to the back.
* The old standby, the crochet hook, works too.

Getting the wrinkles out

* At home or away you can get the wrinkles out of garments quickly. Hang your garment on the back of the bathroom door. Turn the shower on -- hot! Close the bathroom door. Allow 10-20 minutes -- enough time for the steam to penetrate the fibers.

Buttons

* When you lose a button from a blouse or shirt you can often find one elsewhere on the garment. If you never button the top button anyway, take it and use it for a replacement. If the bottom button is hidden from view because you keep it tucked in, take it away and use it for the replacement (you can sew on something similar). Maybe you will find extra buttons on the cuff. Whatever you do, there's no point buying a whole new set of buttons if you don't have to!

Hints to remember:

Gift Planning Guides
Clothing Guide

Item	Name / Size	Name / Size	Name / Size	Name / Size	Name / Size
Belt					
Blouse/Shirt					
Coat/Jacket					
Dress					
Gloves/Mittens					
Hat/Cap					
Lingerie					
Pajamas					
Slacks					
Socks					
Suit					
Sweater					
Birthday					
Favorite color					
Allergies					

Flowers and Birthstones

Month	Flower	Birthstone
January	White carnation	Garnet
February	Violet	Amethyst
March	Daffodil	Bloodstone/Aquamarine.
April	Daisy	Diamond
May	Lily of the valley	Emerald
June	Red rose	Pearl
July	Larkspur	Ruby
August	Poppy	Sardonyx
September	Aster	Sapphire
October	Calendula	Opal
November	Chrysanthemum	Topaz
December	Holly	Turquoise

Signs of the zodiac

Sign	Dates*	Symbol
Aries	Mar. 21-Apr. 19	Ram
Taurus	Apr. 20-May 20	Bull
Gemini	May 21-June 20	Twins
Cancer	June 21-July 22	Crab
Leo	July 23-Aug. 22	Lion
Virgo	Aug. 23-Sept. 22	Virgin
Libra	Sept. 23-Oct. 23	Scales
Scorpio	Oct. 24-Nov. 22	Scorpion
Sagittarius	Nov. 23-Dec. 21	Archer
Capricorn	Dec. 22-Jan. 19	Goat
Aquarius	Jan. 20-Feb. 19	Water bearer
Pisces	Feb. 20-Mar. 20	Fishes

*Dates may vary by one day depending on the year of birth.

State flowers

State	Flower
Alabama	Camellia
Alaska	Forget-me-not
Arizona	Saquaro cactus
Arkansas	Apple blossom
California	Golden poppy
Colorado	Columbine
Connecticut	Mountain laurel
Delaware	Peach blossom
Florida	Orange blossom
Georgia	Cherokee rose
Hawaii	Hibiscus
Idaho	Mock orange
Illinois	Violets
Indiana	Peony
Iowa	Wild rose
Kansas	Sunflower
Kentucky	Goldenrod
Louisiana	Magnolia
Maine	White pine cone & tassel
Maryland	Black-eyed susan
Massachusetts	Mayflower
Michigan	Wild crab apple
Minnesota	Lady slipper
Mississippi	Magnolia
Missouri	Hawthorn
Montana	Bitterroot
Nebraska	Goldenrod
Nevada	Sagebrush
New Hampshire	Lilac
New Jersey	Purple violet
New Mexico	Yucca
New York	Wild rose
North Carolina	Dogwood
North Dakota	Wild prairie rose
Ohio	Scarlet carnation
Oklahoma	Mistletoe
Oregon	Oregon grape
Pennsylvania	Mountain laurel
Rhode Island	Violet
South Carolina	Yellow jessamine
South Dakota	Pasqueflower
Tennessee	Iris
Texas	Blue bonnet
Utah	Sego lily
Vermont	Red clover
Virginia	Dogwood
Washington	Wild rhododendron
West Virginia	Great rhododendron
Wisconsin	Violet
Wyoming	Indian paintbrush

Index

Decorate the easy way...

with over 1,000
Iron-on Transfer Designs
for ONLY 1¢ EACH

Perfect for Crewel,
Applique,
Embroidery,
Needlepoint,
Tole and
Ball Point Paints, **or...**

NEW
**Improved Toolset
Yarn Size Needle
Included**

...Use the Amazing NEEDLEPUNCH™
with the **unique** turn-screw adjustment that
creates plush pile embroidery up to 1/2" high.
Textures go from a short tight nap to rich shag pile
by simply turning a screw. Cuts embroidery time in half.
Use ordinary floss to decorate blouses, wallhangings
or quilts. Add your personal touch to linens or gifts.

OUR GIFT TO YOU
To help you get started, we'll include with your
NEEDLEPUNCH™ our 24 page craft booklet
with lots of good ideas to follow.

CRAFTWAYS Dept. N21
1465 Fourth Street
Berkeley, CA 94710-1374

NEEDLEPUNCH™ toolset comes in three needle
sizes for **$3.50** each:
☐ 1-strand, ☐ 3-strand, ☐ Yarn size
Order all three sizes and work with a variety of
fabrics and threads for ONLY ☐ **$6.99**

☐ 6" Screw-tightened hoop **$1.50**
☐ No-smudge transfer pencil **$1.65**

Add $1.50 shipping + 6% tax in CA.

Name

Address

City   State   Zip

Each book contains over
100 reusable transfers for just **$2.50** per book:

☐ American Flowers ☐ Kids & Bubblegum
☐ For the Holidays ☐ Designs for Little Ones
☐ Birds & Butterflies ☐ Designs of Many Lands
☐ Kitchen Collection ☐ Alphabets & Samplers
☐ Just Flowers ☐ Peasant & Folk Designs
Order the entire 1,000 design collection
☐ **The Big Book of 10 ($25 value) only $9.99**

Send us your very best hints:

Why not share your needlecraft hints with other interested readers?

Send us your original hints,shortcuts, and general needlecraft discoveries...as many as you like. And, if we decide to use one or more of your ideas in our next "Hints" book, we'll credit you in print as the originator of the hint. You'll receive written notice from us that we're going to use your hint. Submission of a hint by a reader constitutes permission for accepted hints to be published in any revised "Mary Ann's Best of Needlecraft Hints."

Send your hints to:
Craftways Corporation
Publishing Division Attn: Mary Ann
1465 Fourth St.
Berkeley, Ca. 94710-1374

P.S. You'll also receive a complimentary copy of the edition in which your hints appear.

Let us help solve your gift giving problems:

Just think of all the people you know who would really enjoy receiving a copy of "Mary Ann's Best of Needlecraft Hints." It's the perfect gift for people, who like you, are resourceful and enjoy needlecraft projects

We'll send a copy as a gift from you. Simply fill in and send us the coupon below and we'll immediately ship a "Hints Book" in your name.
Send $4.99 for each book (check or money order). Please include $1.00 for shipping and handling.

From:
Name _____
Address _____
City_____State_____Zip_____

Ship to:
Name _____
Address _____
City_____State_____Zip_____

Ship to:
Name _____
Address _____
City_____State_____Zip_____

Ship to:
Name _____
Address _____
City_____State_____Zip_____